The One Ann Only

Some quotes herein were spoken by Ann Richards but may
not be original to her or her speechwriting staff.

ISBN 978-1-4773-2592-6

doi: 10.7560/325926

Designed by DJ Stout and Michelle Maudet, Pentagram Austin.
Photo editing and research by Margaret Justus and Lynne Dobson.
Printed in Allen, Texas, in an edition of 5,000 by ColorDynamics.

Distributed by the University of Texas Press
www.utpress.utexas.edu

The One Ann Only

Wit and Wisdom from Texas Governor Ann Richards

Foreword by Sarah Bird

1933

Dorothy Ann Willis is born September 1 to Cecil and Iona Willis in Lacy Lakeview, north of Waco, Texas.

1945 Attends Theodore Roosevelt Junior High School in San Diego, California, while her father serves in the Navy. From her memoir, "Going to California at that time was like going to a foreign country. There were kids of different colors who came from different backgrounds but who were just like me. I was never able to understand racial prejudice after that."

1946 Enters Waco High School, drops her first name, and calls herself "Ann."

1949 Attends Girls State, the annual mock legislative assembly, and is elected as one of two Texas delegates to Girls Nation, in Washington, D.C.

1950 Graduates high school and attends Baylor University on a debate scholarship.

1953 Marries her high-school sweetheart, David Richards, who later becomes a noted civil rights lawyer. Together they raise four children: Cecile, Dan, Clark, and Ellen. The couple divorces in 1984.

1954 Graduates from Baylor University with a Bachelor of Arts degree in speech, then earns her teaching certificate from the University of Texas at Austin.

1956 Teaches social studies and history at Fulmore Junior High School in Austin for several years.

Early 1970s Volunteers in numerous political campaigns and runs races to elect the first women state representatives from Travis County, Sarah Weddington and Wilhelmina Delco. Later serves as legislative aide to Weddington, who will successfully argue the *Roe v. Wade* abortion rights case before the U.S. Supreme Court. While on Weddington's staff, Richards works to extend the rights of women to get financial credit on their own, without the permission of a spouse or male guardian.

1976 Defeats a three-term incumbent to become the first woman elected to the Travis County Commissioners Court. She is reelected to a second term.

1976 Becomes a founding board member of the Foundation for Women's Resources, which creates the Texas Women's History Project and Exhibition, one of the first of its kind in the nation. Later she helps organize the foundation's landmark program, Leadership Texas, which for more than 30 years has mentored hundreds of women leaders throughout Texas.

1977 Leads the Texas delegation to the National Women's Conference in Houston to celebrate the International Year of the Woman.

1980 Completes treatment for alcoholism and spends the rest of her life helping others who have problems with addiction.

1982 Is elected Texas state treasurer, becoming the first woman to win a statewide office in more than fifty years. She reorganizes and modernizes the financial operations and management of billions of dollars in state revenue. In 1986, she wins a second term.

1988 Delivers the widely heralded keynote address to the Democratic National Convention in Atlanta and becomes recognized as a national political figure.

1989 Publishes her memoir, *Straight from the Heart: My Life in Politics and Other Places.*

1990 Wins the Democratic gubernatorial nomination, defeating attorney general and former congressman Jim Mattox and former governor Mark White.

1990 Is elected the first woman Texas governor in her own

right, defeating Clayton Williams, a Republican millionaire rancher from West Texas, by a margin of 49 to 47 percent.

1991–1995 Establishes a record as one of the most popular and progressive governors in Texas history. Some of her notable accomplishments include:

- Appoints an unprecedented number of women and people of color to serve in state government. Of her nearly 3,000 appointments, 46 percent are female, 15 percent are Black, 20 percent are Hispanic, and 2 percent are Asian American. She appoints the first African Americans to the University of Texas Board of Regents and the Texas Department of Commerce Policy Board. She names the first crime survivor to the state criminal justice board, the first person with a disability to the Texas Health and Human Services Board, and the first teacher to chair the State Board of Education.
- Conducts unscheduled visits on substandard nursing homes to highlight abuses and force significant changes in how the state regulates conditions in nursing homes to care for the state's ill and elderly citizens.
- Attracts many new businesses to Texas, including AT&T's national headquarters to San Antonio. She expands the movie industry in the state and through the Texas Film Commission brings new productions to Texas. Despite a national recession, under her leadership the Texas economy grows by 2 percent.
- Leads reform of the Texas prison system, including establishing the first substance-abuse program for inmates, and embarks on a prison-building program to expand facilities to house violent offenders.
- Works to reduce gun violence by vetoing legislation that would allow Texans to carry concealed handguns inside public establishments without the business owner's permission.
- Reforms the rate-setting process at the State Board of Insurance to make it more fair to consumers.
- Protects the Edwards Aquifer, a major source of water for Central Texas, and directs her appointees at major

state boards and commissions to prevent toxic runoff into Texas rivers and streams.
- Institutes a statewide ethics reform program for all state employees and appoints former congresswoman Barbara Jordan as her ethics advisor.
- Works with the legislature to create the Texas Lottery and signs the bill into law.
- Celebrates her 60th birthday by earning her motorcycle driver's license.
- Hosts numerous national and international leaders, including Queen Elizabeth II of England and her husband, Prince Phillip, the Duke of Edinburgh, during a state visit to the United States.

1994 Runs for reelection and is defeated by George W. Bush, the same year Republicans win majorities in both houses of Congress for the first time in 40 years.

1995–2001 Serves as consulting advisor to Verner Liipfert Bernhard McPherson & Hand, a Washington, D.C.–based law firm.

2001–2006 Serves as consulting advisor to Public Strategies, Inc., a public affairs firm with offices in Austin and New York, while continuing to campaign for Democratic candidates and social causes, including the protection of women's reproductive rights.

2001 Guest stars in the Texas-themed animated TV series King of the Hill.

2006 Helps create the Ann Richards School for Young Women Leaders, a public, all-girls college-preparatory school in Austin (grades 6-12), which opened in the fall of 2007 and is nationally recognized for its focus on leadership, college readiness, project-based learning, and STEM (Science, Technology, Engineering, and Math).

2006

On September 13, after a six-month battle with esophageal cancer, dies at her home in Austin. Her remains are interred at the Texas State Cemetery in Austin, next to her longtime companion, author Edwin "Bud" Shrake.

Dorothy Ann's Double Strength Sass

By Sarah Bird

What was it about Ann Richards? What was the essence of her One Ann Only–ness? How did a recovering alcoholic divorcée with four children and a low-profile job as the state treasurer of Texas steal America's heart from the very first moment she appeared on national television? And how has she remained so beloved all these decades later?

Let's go back to that galvanizing debut.

The year was 1988.

It was a steamy July night in Atlanta. The Democrats had convened to select a candidate to run against the incumbent vice president, George H. W. Bush. At the top of a slate of contenders was the preordained nominee, the luckless Michael Dukakis. The convention desperately needed a jolt of energy, and an unknown state treasurer took the podium and zapped it with a lightning bolt of a keynote address so electrifying that on the American Rhetoric list of top 100 speeches of the twentieth century, Ann's address claims the 38th spot. Right behind JFK's plea to stop the nuclear arms race.

Why was that speech so electrifying?

Was it the way she lit up the screen with those eyes as blue and blistering as the flame of an acetylene torch? Was it that unmistakable tornado of white hair? Could it have been the irresistible genuineness of her throaty Texas drawl? Was it that Ann—not just an ardent and unapologetic feminist but an outspoken advocate for choice—managed to appeal as strongly to men as she did to all us women who had long hungered for exactly her brand of high-octane estrogen?

Yes.

Yes to all that.

Though it is futile to attempt to dissect charisma, we try anyway to answer these questions: How did Dorothy Ann Willis, born on September 1, 1933, in Lacy Lakeview, Texas, become the first woman in her own right—sorry, Ma, but being a stand-in for Pa doesn't count—to be elected governor of Texas? And how did she succeed in opening government to more people of the non-white and nonmale persuasion than ever before in the state's history?

What did Ann have that no other female politician before and, arguably since, has been able to duplicate? How did she beat the good ol' boys at their own game?

Some credit for Ann's dazzling oratory skills must be given to her time on the Waco High School debate team, where she shone brightly enough to win a scholarship to Baylor University. But we all know debate nerds with the charisma of a doorknob. No, the one element that can't be either quantified or underestimated, the one that we celebrate in these pages, is the magic of Ann's humor.

What truly won us over back in 1988 was the fact that Ann possessed that rarest of qualities in a politician: an actual functioning sense of humor. She brought down the convention house, joking about old dogs that wouldn't hunt and Ginger Rogers doing everything Fred Astaire did. Backwards and in high heels. But she blew the roof off the place when, with impeccable timing and mock sorrowfulness, she lamented, "Poor George. He can't help it. He was born with a silver foot in his mouth."

Though my life growing up on military bases around the globe could not have been more different from little Dorothy Ann's, our worlds had this in common: They were masculine in the extreme. But one secret counterweight had the power to tip those scales in a girl's favor, and that was a well-timed wisecrack.

Ann, born in the worst year of the worst depression this country has ever endured, grew up in a hardscrabble time in a hardscrabble place where girls may have been even more extraneous than they were on the overseas military bases of my young years. By and large, girls like Ann and me had two missions in life: to be cute and to be quiet. There were no dispensations from being cute, but there was a tiny loophole in the Be Quiet mandate. A girl could speak her mind if—and only if—she got a laugh. Dorothy Ann discovered that loophole and,

armed with every country zinger and her own dose of double strength sass, leaped right through it.

Ann learned the power of the well-aimed barb both to disarm and to charm. But what elevated Ann's wit to a realm where it sung rather than stung was her irrefutable, ironclad realness.

I did not try to deconstruct the elements of her bred-in-the-bone authenticity until September 13, 2006, when, gutted by grief that one of the guiding lights of my life had been extinguished, I could not stop staring at the photos that accompanied Ann's obituary. Along with mourners around the world, I fell again under the spell of those eyes, that hair, that smile.

This fixation on a woman's appearance is wrong. It was wrong then and it's wrong now. Wrong though it might have been, it was and still is the harsh barometer by which women in the public eye are judged. Since that goes double for Southern women, the choices Ann made in that department reveal substance as much as style. Which is why I ended up zooming in on her glorious and gloriously uncorrected collection of shar-pei-quality neck wrinkles. It was there, written within their creased calligraphy, that I found the key to understanding Ann's one-and-only realness: Real Texas Women don't hide what God has furrowed. If neck wrinkles bother a Real Texas Woman, I surmised, she will go out, find the best plastic surgeon around, have the damn facelift, and throw a party to show off her new profile.

Or she will get herself something a whole hell of a lot bigger to worry about. Like taming a frontier or busting up the white boys' club that had occupied the Texas statehouse since Reconstruction.

A Real Texas Woman like Ann took the wrinkles and the sags, the wattles and the bags, for the extremely useful reminders that they are—that at this great banquet of life, those of us wondering (a) where we put our reading glasses and (b) why we were looking for them in the first place are a lot closer to the dessert cart than to the pupu platter. And we should use the time we have been given accordingly.

Heartbroken by her passing, I was wondering how Ann had actually felt about those wrinkles, when bobbing on the ocean of ink that poured out to celebrate her life and mourn her death came an answer to my question. Rena Pedersen, formerly the editorial page editor at the *Dallas Morning News,* recalled the last time she had seen the governor:

> During the Q and A, Ann was complimented about her appearances as a political commentator and asked why she didn't have a TV program. Without hesitation, she grabbed the folds of skin under her chin and flapped them with her hand. "They don't want you on TV with this," she said. When asked why she didn't just have plastic surgery, Ann replied, "I don't think that's the kind of example I want to set for my granddaughter."

Ann was a beautiful woman who used her beauty not as a meal ticket but as a cautionary tale. After opening so many doors that no woman before her had even cracked, she was ever mindful that those who followed her must be properly equipped to succeed.

Enter the Kilgore Rangerettes.

Every year the famous collegiate dancing drill team came to Austin, and all 40 or so of them in their white-hat, white-booted cowgirl outfits, acres of leg on display, would line up Rockettes-style in the reception room for a photo op with the governor. Perhaps it was the title of a famous documentary that had been made about the group, *Beauty Knows No Pain,* that caused Ann to suspect these young women might need a bit of guidance on that exact subject.

A Kilgore Rangerette reaches up to shake hands with Governor Ann Richards, who greets thousands of jubilant Texans along the inaugural parade route on January 15, 1991.

Whatever Ann's inspiration, Margaret Justus, her deputy press secretary from 1989 to 1994, remembers one visit when Ann shared this bit of wisdom with the comely young women: "Someday your face will look like mine, so stay focused on finishing your education so you can go after your dreams."

Texas women don't get any more real than that.

Writing this tribute has made me miss Ann so much that I went in search of comfort and, perhaps, reassurance that I was not exaggerating her magnetic singularity. Online, I found both in the wealth of videos from her many television appearances. All those recordings make it as clear as it had been in Atlanta that I had not overestimated just how telegenic the woman was. It took only a few minutes of viewing for the truth to become obvious: Though we have now had decades of politicos buffed up to a high gloss with media training, no one since Ann has equaled her ability to reach through the lens of a television camera and become as immediate and real to viewers as any person in their life.

Even beaming in from the pixelated ether, Ann was exactly who she had always been: an approachable, compassionate woman. One who would stay until the last hand was shaken and every question had been answered. Particularly if that question was being asked by a woman or a person of color.

Ann's One Ann Only–ness was on particularly full and splendid display in a broadcast from the night of the 1992 presidential election. Bush the Elder was running against Bill Clinton. ABC news anchor Peter Jennings was monitoring the returns, when he announced in his ultra-urbane Canadian accent that a special guest was joining him.

And then there she was, lighting up the screen.

"Good evening, Governor," Jennings intoned solemnly.

"How are ya?" Ann asked in her great gravelly drawl, as casual and as unimpressed as any rancher from her parents' hometowns of Hogjaw and Bug Tussle greeting a neighbor across the fence.

Jennings answered with a tight, unamused smile and then launched in, echoing pundits' predictions that third-party candidate Ross Perot would split the vote and allow Bush to win Texas.

Ann interrupted Jennings with an earthy get-real chuckle, the chastising finger waggle of the schoolteacher she had once been, and this guarantee, "Ah, no, no, no, Peter, we gon' *win* Texas tonight."

Then Ann proceeded to blind us with the biggest cat-that-ate-the-canary grin the world has ever seen, and foreclosing any further discussion of a Democratic rout, she signed off, "Great to talk to y'all!"

As always, Ann had gotten the last word. And, praise Jesus, that word was "y'all," delivered with an amused benevolence that bordered on condescension but was still as warm as butter on a hot biscuit.

If only it had been the last word on Texas politics.

But, as we all know, it wasn't. Texas did not go for Clinton in 1992. Nor has any other Democratic presidential candidate carried our state since the peanut farmer from Georgia in 1976.

And Ann? Ann was both our last female governor and for three long decades the last Democrat elected to the office.

That is a puzzling fact, considering all that her administration managed to accomplish in the face of a deeply obstructionist legislature. Such as? Such as helping to solve the state's education crisis. Attracting many new businesses and keeping several major ones, like General Motors, from leaving. Championing the environment, the arts, and prison reform.

But more than those concrete achievements, Ann—twice elected as the first woman in office as both a Travis County commissioner and a state treasurer—changed forever our idea of who could, who should, be running the state of Texas.

As I write this, the ink is still drying on the voter suppression bill that the current occupant of the statehouse signed just a few minutes ago. I am heartsick at seeing Ann's beloved Texas transformed into a carnival of political outrages, with rides such as the life-threatening Handmaid's Tale Tilt-A-Whirl and that all-time favorite, Back to the Past!, where a power-hungry legislature reanimates the corpse of Jim Crow and ensures that Texas will remain the hardest state in the union for citizens to exercise their fundamental right to vote.

Small wonder that those too-brief transformative years—when Ann made government look a heck of a lot more like the people it represented—continue to shimmer in our memories like JFK's Camelot. It's why we turn to each other, shaking our heads at the latest desecration of democracy, dizzied by the cynical cravenness of this descent into partisan madness, and ask, "What would Ann say?"

We know for a fact that, whatever her precise words might be, the one thing they would not be is defeatist. Not when the will of the people is being so blatantly, so brutally, subverted. Forged during the Great Depression and tempered by the crucible years of World War II, Ann had a case-hardened faith in her people. In Texans. In our ultimate fairness and resilience.

Whatever Ann's message might have been, you are holding the proof that she would have delivered it with heart, with humor, and—most vital for our troubled times—with hope.

So, I invite you to turn the pages and let yourself be infused once again with Ann's toughness, with her essential Texas grit. Let yourself feel the spark from those acetylene-torch eyes; let them light you up. And then, like Ann, put your faith in the people and never stop fighting. Because, not today, maybe not tomorrow, but one day a whole lot sooner than the current carnival masters think, it is going to happen . . .

We *gon'* win Texas.

Y'all.

Richards waves to the crowd before her inauguration. The Paramount Theatre marquee salutes her campaign slogan, "The New Texas"—Richards's vision of an honest and more inclusive state government.

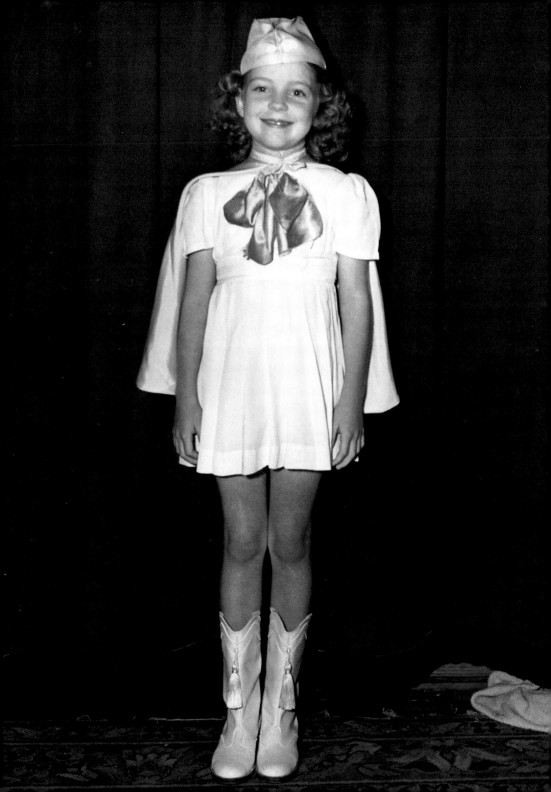

I have very strong feelings about how you lead your life. Always look ahead and never look back.

One of the most valuable lessons I learned . . . is that we all have to learn from our mistakes, and we learn from those mistakes a lot more than we learn from the things we succeeded in doing.

I have always had the feeling I could do anything, and my dad told me I could. I was in college before I found out he might be wrong.

There are real people with real lives who are counting on us. And we will not—we cannot— disappoint them.

Women, it was painfully clear, weren't going to be allowed to use their brains, and I certainly wanted to use mine.

I get a lot of cracks about my hair, mostly from men who don't have any.

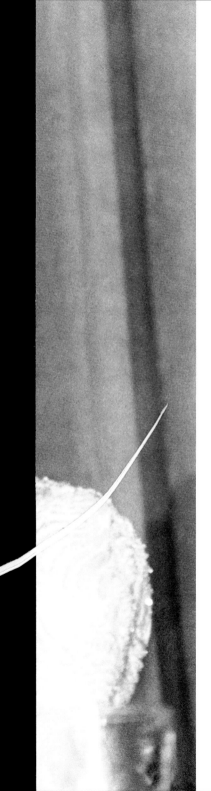

You bet being funny helps accomplish things. I've always maintained that people don't realize how many brain cells it takes to be funny. And politics ought to be fun—after baseball, it's our next favorite national pastime.

Learn to enjoy your own company. You are the one person you can count on living with for the rest of your life.

The public does not like you to mislead or represent yourself to be something you're not. And the other thing that the public really does like is the self-examination to say, you know, I'm not perfect. I'm just like you. They don't ask their public officials to be perfect. They just ask them to be smart, truthful, honest, and show a modicum of good sense.

I've been tested by fire and the fire lost.

There is a special mystique to Texas. Texans represent many things to the uninitiated: We are bigger than life in our boots and Stetsons, rugged individualists whose two-steppin' has achieved world-wide acclaim, and we were the first to define hospitality.

I feel very
strongly
that change
is good
because it
stirs up the
system.

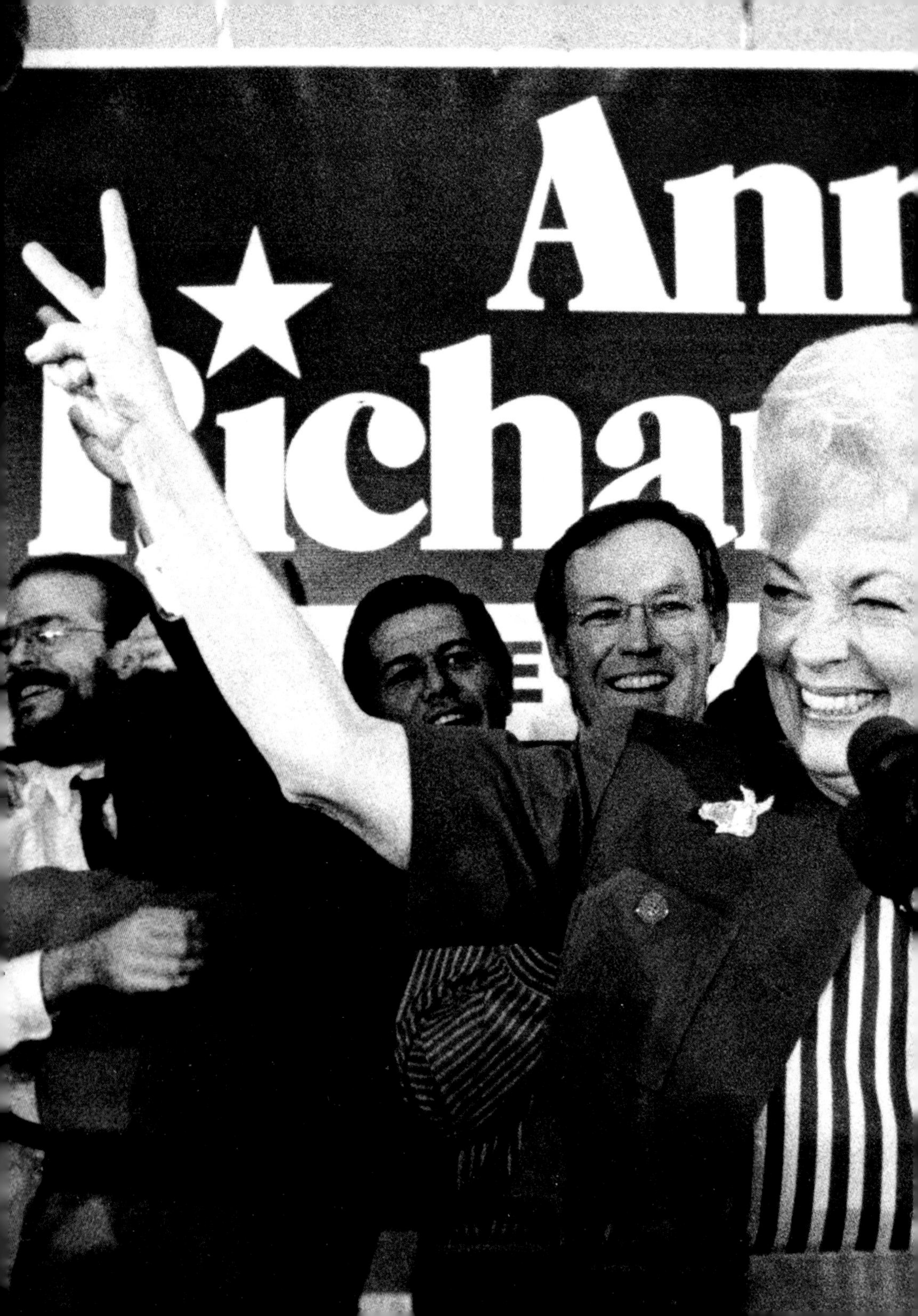

Ginger Rogers did everything Fred Astaire did. She just did it backwards and in high heels.

Cherish your friends and family as if your life depended on it. Because it does.

I believe in
recovery, and I
believe as a role
model I have the
responsibility
to let young
people know you
can make a
mistake and come
back from it.

Sobriety has freed me to deal with failure and never give up.

I want to urge you
to make waves.
I want to urge
you to rock the
boat. … I want you
to speak out at
whatever cost if it
comes from your
heart. You are
going to build this
country in which
my grandchildren
will grow up, and
I hope that you
are proud of it.

I wanted to say,
I realize that I am
female and that not
many females get to
do what I am doing,
but I hope you
will listen to me.

If I could have any impact on our culture, it would be for women to have self-confidence, to have self-esteem, to see their value and then act on it—whatever their value or talent is.

I have seen the very bottom of life: I was so afraid I wouldn't be funny anymore. I just knew that I would lose my zaniness and my sense of humor. But I didn't. Recovery turned out to be a wonderful thing.

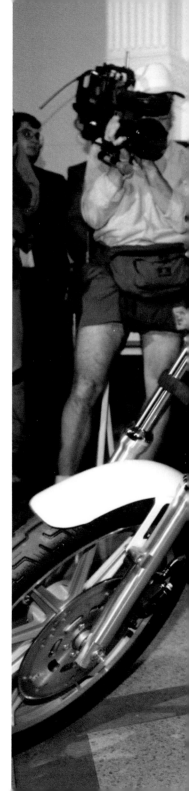

If you think taking care of yourself is selfish, change your mind.

A road to a friend's house is never long.

The Reverend Martin Luther King, Jr. who was born on this day, said we have come this far on the strength of a dream.

Now our challenge is to transform that dream into reality . . . to fill the pages of history with the story of Texans who came into office envisioning a new era of greatness . . . and breathed life into that vision.

Today, we have a vision of a Texas where opportunity knows no race, no gender, no color—a glimpse of the possibilities of what can happen in government if we simply open the doors and let the people in.

Tomorrow, we have to build that Texas.

Today, we have a vision of a Texas with clean air and land and water . . . a Texas where a strong economy lives in harmony with a safe environment...

Today, we have a vision of a Texas where every child receives an education that allows them to claim the full promise of their lives...

Today, we have a vision of a Texas where every citizen is treated by the government with respect and dignity and honesty . . . where consumers are protected . . . where business is nurtured and valued . . . where good jobs are plentiful . . . where those in need find compassion and love and help where every decision is measured against a high standard of ethics and true commitment to the public trust.

Tomorrow we've got to get about building that Texas.

— January 15, 1991 Inaugural Address

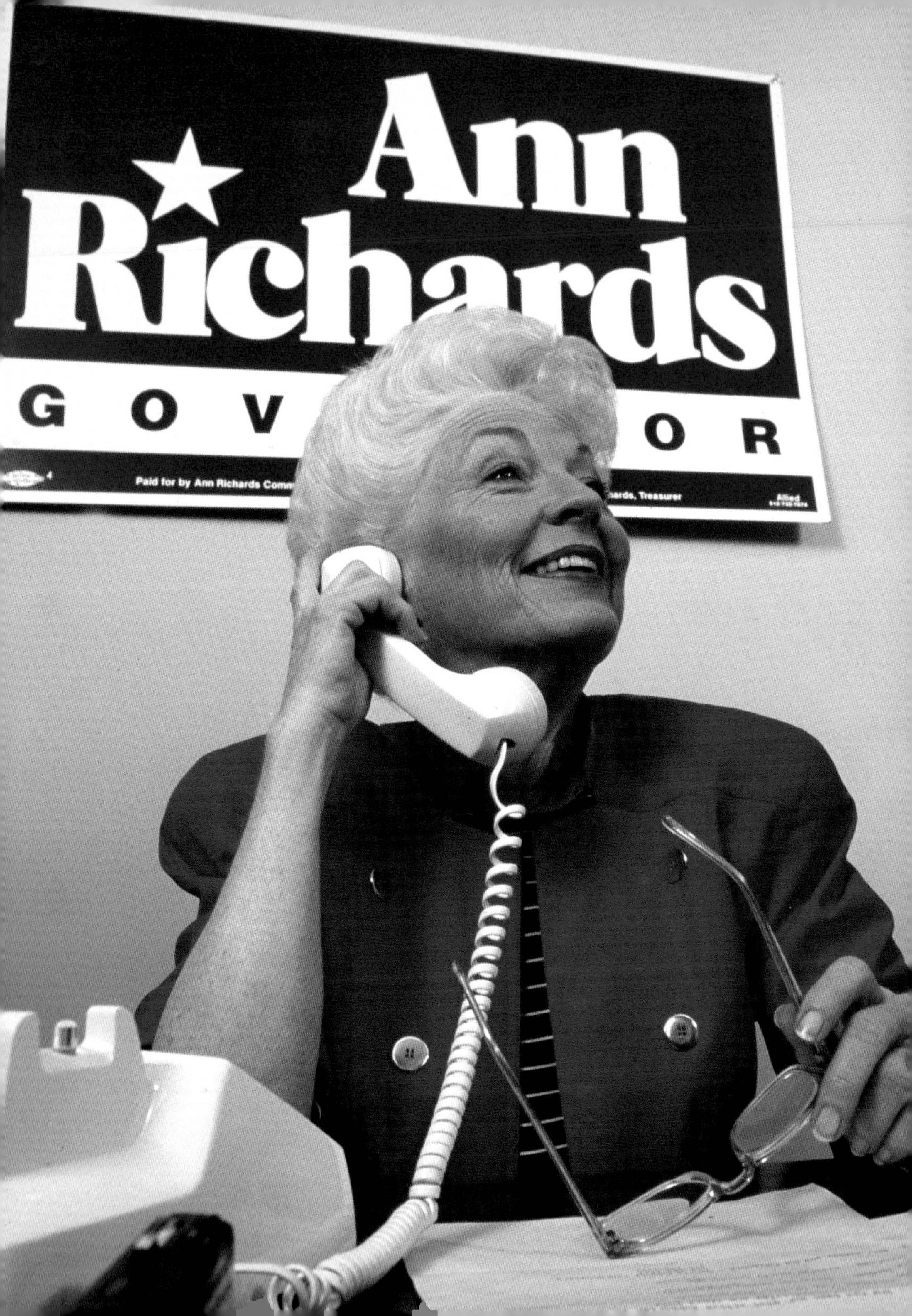
Ann
Richards
GOV
OR

I am not afraid to shake up the system, and government needs more shaking up than any other system I know.

Teaching was the hardest work I had ever done, including being governor of Texas.

THE NEW TEXAS
Ann Richards

You can get
a lot done
if you don't
care who gets
the credit.

Today I am asking you to hold on to that sense of purpose and shared responsibility. Because the people who sent us here want leadership, not partisanship. They want to know that we get up every morning and go to work—not to lay a predicate for the next election ... but to lay a foundation for a stronger Texas.

— 1992 State of the State Address

I thought I knew Texas pretty well, but I had no notion of its size until I campaigned it.

I don't know
exactly when
I came to
feminism.
Somewhere
I knew
women ought
to be able to
do anything.

Life isn't fair, but government absolutely must be.

We're not going to have the America that we want until we elect leaders who are going to tell the truth—not most days but every day.

Ann
chards
VERNOR

for by Ann Richards Committee, P.O. Box 12404, Austin, TX 78711, (512) 476-5151, Dan Richards, Treasurer

I'd like them to remember me by saying, "She opened government to everyone."

I think you have
to deal with grief in
the sense that you
have to recognize
that you have it and
say that it's okay to
have all the sadness.

I wonder if she'll ever grasp the changes I've seen in my life—if she'll ever believe that there was a time when Blacks could not drink from public water fountains, when Hispanic children were punished for speaking Spanish in the public schools and women couldn't vote. I want so much to tell Lily how far we've come, you and I. And as the ball rolls back and forth, I want to tell her how very lucky she is. That, for all of our differences, we are still the greatest nation on this good earth. And our strength lies in the men and women who go to work every day, who struggle to balance their family and their jobs, and who should never, ever be forgotten. I just hope that, like her grandparents and her great-grandparents before, Lily goes on to raise her kids with the promise that echoes in homes all across America: that we can do better.

— 1988 Democratic National Convention Keynote Address

What Would Ann Say?

By Mary Beth Rogers

During times of political crisis and turmoil, many of us ask, "What would Ann say?"

Now, more than thirty years after Ann Richards was inaugurated as the 45th governor of Texas, on January 15, 1991, we have a few of her wise and witty answers to that question.

This book brings back powerful memories for me. I was lucky enough to have been "in the room" with Ann Richards so many times when she mused about politics and life with her unique sense of humor and penetrating insight. And I loved being with her when she gave speeches that inspired and brought joy to people all over the nation. I even had the opportunity to run both of her gubernatorial campaigns and to serve as her chief of staff while she was in office.

The One Ann Only collection of photos and words of Ann Richards, as well as the huge red, white, and blue Ann banners that graced our major Texas cities, gives a new generation the opportunity to know about one of the most impactful political leaders in Texas history.

In early 2020, Margaret Justus created the Ann Richards Legacy Project to keep Ann's memory and words alive. When faced with the roadblocks laid down by COVID-19 that prevented large public gatherings, she envisioned colorful banners with images of Ann and her quotes displayed along Congress Avenue in Austin, where the Governor Richards's inaugural parade had been jubilantly celebrated.

Margaret is a former journalist who served as Richards's deputy press secretary from 1989 to 1994. She connected with Molly Alexander at the Downtown Austin Alliance Foundation, and their collaboration led to those banners flying in view of the Texas Capitol. She then brought the project to Dallas, El Paso, Houston, and San Antonio, and more than 300 banners have now been flown across Texas.

The book *The One Ann Only* was the notion of Austin philanthropists Lynne Dobson, a former photojournalist who now uses her photography skills for humanitarian organizations in East Africa, and her husband, Greg Wooldridge, a former newspaper journalist and editor. Inspired by the Ann banners, they worked with Margaret and DJ Stout's Pentagram design team to bring this treasure of Ann's words and deeds to life. Lynne enlisted her friend, Austin novelist Sarah Bird, to capture the essence of Ann's grit and humor in the foreword.

I am deeply grateful to all of those who remind us of the power of Ann's oratory and achievements and her desire to make life better for all of us. She certainly made our lives more interesting and a lot more fun.

Ann's children—Cecile, Dan, Clark, and Ellen—have continued over the years to enhance their mother's legacy through their support of this project and their commitment to the Ann Richards School for Young Women Leaders in Austin.

We want to thank some of Ann's former staffers and friends and others who have helped bring these projects to fruition. They include Raph Bemporad, Cathy Bonner, John Burnett, Sandra Castellanos, Barbara Chapman, Bill Cryer, Deece Eckstein, Fred Ellis, Katherine Gregor, Joene Grissom, Jacquline Justice, Shawn Morris, Kristy Ozmun, Casey Chapman Ross, Gary Scharrer, Mandi Thomas, Lena Thompson, Kirk Watson, Mariah Justus White, Anne Wynne, and Holland Taylor, who wrote and starred in the fabulous one-woman stage show about Governor Richards.

We are also grateful for the indomitable Suzanne Coleman, who worked tirelessly with the governor to create her unforgettable speeches. Even though she is no longer with us, Suzanne would have been ecstatic to see her boss's words

celebrated for all to appreciate.

Special thanks also go to local donors and various organizations that helped bring the Ann banners to their cities: City Councilwomen Natasha Harper-Madison and Kathie Tovo, the Downtown Austin Alliance Foundation, the Winker Family Foundation, and the Tejemos Foundation in Austin; Mayor Eric Johnson, Downtown Dallas Inc., Ambassador Marc Stanley, and Ambassador Ron Kirk in Dallas; City Representative Alexsandra Annello, the El Paso Management District, Deborah Kastrin, and Matthew Ibarra in El Paso; Mayor Sylvester Turner, U.S. Federal

District Judge Vanessa Gilmore, County Judge Lina Hidalgo, Commissioner Rodney Ellis, former Houston Mayor Pro Tem Ellen Cohen, David Ellison, Mary Benton, Angie Bertinot, and the Downtown District in Houston; and Mayor Ron Nirenberg, Patricia Smothers, and Bruce Davidson in San Antonio.

We also want to thank the Austin History Center, the Dolph Briscoe Center for American History, Kilgore College Rangerettes and the Rangerette Showcase, the staff at the University of Texas Press, and all the photographers whose names appear in the photo credits on pages 138-141. Proceeds from the sale of this book will go toward a permanent public tribute in Austin to the one and only Ann Richards.

Top: Actor Holland Taylor immersed herself in the role of her play, *Ann,* which premiered in 2010. The production sold out across the country, including on Broadway and can be seen on the PBS *Great Performances* online platform.

Left: Suzanne Coleman (d. 2017) served as Richards's speechwriter for more than 20 years. In an interview for *Texas Monthly* magazine in 2006, Coleman said, "A good speech isn't necessarily good writing. You have to have timing and tone. Nobody is a better judge of an audience than Ann Richards."

The "Ann banners" displayed in various Texas cities throughout 2021 commemorate the state's 45th governor 30 years after her inauguration. *Left:* Margaret Justus, founder of the Ann Richards Legacy Project, in Houston. *Above:* Dallas. *Opposite page, clockwise from top left:* Austin, San Antonio, Austin, El Paso.

Oh, I would probably have raised more hell.

— Ann's reply when asked what she would
have done differently while in office.

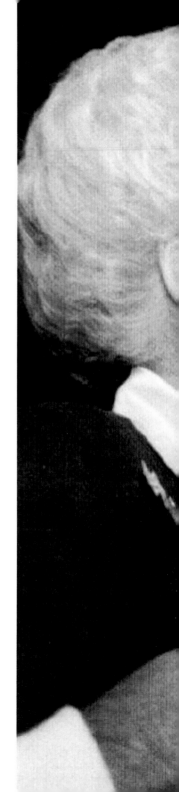

Photo Credits

Cover Pam Francis. Hulton Archive, Getty Images. Richards at the Lincoln Memorial, Washington, D.C., June 4, 1999.

Pages 2–3 Jana Birchum. Richards at a hallway press gaggle, St. Mary's University, San Antonio, Texas, 1994.

Page 5 Jill DiCuffa. Members of the Starfish swim team representing the Ann Richards School for Young Women Leaders, Austin, Texas, 2019.

Page 6 Annie Leibowitz for *Vanity Fair*. South Padre Island, Texas, 1992.

Page 8 Larry Murphy. Ann Richards Papers, di_07843, The Dolph Briscoe Center for American History, The University of Texas at Austin. Hillary Clinton, Ann Richards, and Lady Bird Johnson.

Page 9 Lynne Dobson. Ann Richards's gubernatorial campaign button collection provided by Greg Wooldridge.

Pages 10–11 Ave Bonar. The Dolph Briscoe Center for American History, The University of Texas at Austin, Box 3V224. Richards makes a campaign stop at the Liberty County Courthouse, Liberty, Texas, August 28, 1990.

Page 14 Photographer unknown. A Kilgore Rangerette shakes hands with Governor Richards during inaugural parade, Austin, Texas, January 15, 1991.

Page 17 Richard Carson. Richards walks along Congress Avenue in Austin with her sons, Dan Richards (far right) and Clark Richards (far left), during the People's March to the Texas State Capitol, where thousands of well-wishers from across Texas attended the inaugural celebration, Austin, Texas, January 15, 1991. The Paramount Theatre marquee salutes her campaign slogan, "The New Texas"—Richards's vision of "a Texas where opportunity knows no race, no gender, no color—a glimpse of the possibilities of what can happen in government if we simply open the doors and let the people in."

Page 18 Ellen Richards's personal collection. Young Dorothy Ann Willis, Lacy Lakeview, Texas, ca. 1938.

Pages 20–21 Photographer unknown. Ann Richards Papers, di_00777, The Dolph Briscoe Center for American History, The University of Texas at Austin. Richards (second from left) with her fellow Waco High School debate team members, ca. 1947.

Pages 22–23 Ave Bonar. The Dolph Briscoe Center for American History, The University of Texas at Austin, Box 3V225. Richards with her father, Cecil Willis, during

the production of a television spot in Kyle, Texas, September 14, 1990.

Page 25 Nuri Vallbona. Governor Richards's inauguration ceremony, Texas State Capitol, Austin, Texas, January 15, 1991.

Pages 26–27 Ave Bonar. The Dolph Briscoe Center for American History, The University of Texas at Austin, Box 3V225. Richards displays "A Woman's Place Is in the Dome" T-shirt at her victory celebration, Hyatt Regency Hotel, Austin, Texas, November 6, 1990.

Page 29 Bob Daemmrich. Richards delivers a speech in San Antonio, Texas, 1993.

Pages 30–31 Scott Newton. Ann Richards meets Dolly Parton for the first time, Driskill Hotel, Austin, Texas. July, 1982. Newton recalls he was on a shoot with Travis County Commissioner Richards during her first campaign for state treasurer. "We got word that Dolly, who was in town to promote her new film, *The Best Little Whorehouse in Texas*, wanted to meet Ann. What a scene to witness!" said Newton. "These two women took a delight in each other." Richards and Parton became friends, and Dolly performed at her inauguration in 1991.

Page 32 Bob Daemmrich. Richards hunts dove near

Terrell, Texas, on her 57th birthday, September 1, 1990.

Pages 34–35 Ave Bonar. The Dolph Briscoe Center for American History, The University of Texas at Austin, Box 3V224. Richards with her longtime hairdresser, Gail Huitt, Austin, Texas, August 18,1990. The photo was made for an Operation Hairball campaign mailer to Texas cosmetologists.

Pages 36–37 Maureen Keating. *CQ Roll Call* via Getty Images. Richards laughs as Congressman Charlie Wilson (D-TX) gives remarks at the Independent Action Roast of Gov. Ann Richards dinner in Washington, D.C., June 13, 1991.

Page 39 Ron Galella. Ron Galella Collection, Getty Images. At a party honoring Texas Governor Ann Richards at the Russian Tea Room, New York City, July 14, 1992.

Pages 40–41 Bob Daemmrich. Richards serving as the grand marshal of the Luling Watermelon Thump parade, Luling, Texas, ca. 1993.

Page 43 Ave Bonar. The Dolph Briscoe Center for American History, The University of Texas at Austin, Box 3V224. Richards in a heated exchange with her Democratic primary opponent Jim Mattox, former congressman and then attorney general, at the AFL-CIO COPE Convention, Austin, Texas, January 23, 1990. Richards went on to defeat Mattox in a primary runoff.

Pages 44–45 Wyatt McSpadden for *LIFE* magazine. Richards on a dove hunt, Honey Grove, Texas, 1994.

Page 46 Kirk Tuck. State Treasurer Ann Richards with roses presented by Texas Land Commissioner Gary Mauro after her speech in support of Walter Mondale and Geraldine Ferraro, who were running for president and vice president. Texas State Capitol, Austin, Texas, 1984.

Pages 48–49 Karen Dickey. Photographic Archive, e_kd_0048, The Dolph Briscoe Center for American History, The University of Texas at Austin. Governor Richards declares May 4, 1991, "ZZ Top Day in Texas," Governor's Reception Room, Texas State Capitol, Austin, Texas.

Pages 50–51 Nuri Vallbona. At Richards's inauguration, supporters carry signs reading, "It's Our Turn," Texas State Capitol grounds, Austin, Texas, January 15, 1991.

Pages 52–53 Bob Thomas. UPI Photo, PICB-19746, Austin History Center, Austin Public Library. Richards's

primary election night victory party, Hyatt Regency Hotel, Austin, Texas, April 10, 1990.

Page 55 Wally McNamee. Corbis via Getty Images. State Treasurer Richards delivers the 1988 Democratic National Convention keynote address, Atlanta, Georgia, July 1, 1988.

Page 56 Photographer unknown. Ann Richards Papers, di_04320, The Dolph Briscoe Center for American History, The University of Texas at Austin. Richards (Ann Willis) on the edge of Barton Springs pool with Girls State friends, Austin, Texas, ca. 1947.

Pages 58–59 Photographer unknown. Ann Richards Papers, camh-dob-007359_pub.tif, The Dolph Briscoe Center for American History, The University of Texas at Austin. Richards speaks with middle school students, ca. 1992.

Pages 60–61 Shane Bowen. Ann Richards Papers, di_08620, The Dolph Briscoe Center for American History, The University of Texas at Austin. Richards with her four grandchildren: (left to right) Lily Adams, Hannah Adams, Jennifer Richards, and Daniel Adams, ca. 1992.

Pages 62–63 Ave Bonar. The Dolph Briscoe Center for American History, The

University of Texas at Austin, Box 3V225. Richards having afternoon tea at the Russian Tea Room during a fundraising trip to New York City, September 18,1990.

Page 64 Kenneth C. Zirkel. Richards attends a campaign rally for Jim Hunt, a former North Carolina governor running for reelection, Raleigh, North Carolina, October 18, 1992.

Pages 66–67 Ave Bonar. The Dolph Briscoe Center for American History, The University of Texas at Austin, Box 3V225. Richards greets Liz Carpenter, author and former press secretary to Lady Bird Johnson, on her way to the podium at her gubernatorial victory party, Hyatt Regency Hotel, Austin, Texas, November 6, 1990.

Pages 68–69 Karen Dickey. Photographic Archive, e_kd_0022, The Dolph Briscoe Center for American History, The University of Texas at Austin. Governor Richards signs a Hate Crimes bill in the Governor's Reception Room, Texas State Capitol, Austin, Texas, June 19, 1993.

Page 71 Ave Bonar. Ann Richards Papers, camh-dob-007362, The Dolph Briscoe Center for American History, The University of Texas at Austin. Richards has a campaign lunch with Hispanic supporters at Tio Tito's

restaurant in Austin, Texas, February 2, 1990.

Pages 72–73 Jayne Wexler. Richards photographed with her daughters, Ellen and Cecile Richards, for the book *Daughters and Mothers* by Jayne Wexler and Lauren Cowen, Austin, Texas, 1996.

Pages 74–75 Lisa Davis. AR-2010-022-05-07-016, Austin History Center, Austin Public Library. Richards with former Texas congresswoman Barbara Jordan at a University of Texas Lady Longhorns basketball game, Frank Erwin Center, Austin, Texas, ca. 1990s.

Pages 76–77 Bill Kennedy. Photo 1992/095-2-1, Courtesy of Texas State Library and Archives Commission. Richards receives a Harley-Davidson motorcycle, Governor's Reception Room, Texas State Capitol, Austin, Texas, 1992. Harley-Davidson sent Richards a Harley Hog after she told the Capitol press corps she wanted to learn to ride a motorcycle for her 60th birthday. She later earned her motorcycle license and gave the bike to the Texas Department of Public Safety motorcycle-training program.

Pages 78–79 Peter Turnley. Corbis/VCG via Getty Images. Richards campaigning with President Bill Clinton (center) and U.S. Treasury

Secretary and former U.S. Senator Lloyd Bentsen in Houston, Texas, during President Clinton's 1996 reelection bid against U.S. Senator Bob Dole (R-KS).

Page 80 Ave Bonar. Richards is newly sworn in as Texas state treasurer, Austin, Texas, April 12, 1983.

Pages 82–83 Bob Daemmrich. Richards washes dishes during a trip to Big Bend National Park in West Texas. Standing on her left is Carter Smith, later appointed director of Texas Parks and Wildlife Department, 1992.

Pages 84–85 Photographer unknown. Ann Richards Papers, di_04320, The Dolph Briscoe Center for American History, The University of Texas at Austin. Richards attends an AIDS Walk Austin rally, Texas State Capitol, Austin, Texas.

Page 87 Photographer unknown. Ann Richards Papers, di_00290, The Dolph Briscoe Center for American History, The University of Texas at Austin. Ann Richards and Lady Bird Johnson attend a Bob Krueger for Congress campaign event, ca.1975.

Pages 88–89 Ave Bonar. Richards and her four grandchildren, (left to right), Hannah Adams, Daniel Adams, Jennifer Clark, and Lily Adams, pose

on the Governor's Mansion lawn for a Christmas card, October 24, 1993.

Page 90 Ellen Richards's personal collection. Ann Willis in high school, ca. 1947.

Pages 92–93 Mark Perlstein. The Chronicle Collection, Getty Images. Richards celebrates at her inaugural ball with humorist, author, and political columnist Molly Ivins, Austin, Texas, January 15, 1991.

Page 94 Bob Daemmrich. Richards works the phone banks at her campaign headquarters, Austin, Texas, 1990.

Pages 96–97 Shane Bowen. Ann Richards Papers, di_07726, The Dolph Briscoe Center for American History, The University of Texas at Austin, location and date unknown.

Pages 98–99 Ave Bonar. The Dolph Briscoe Center for American History, The University of Texas at Austin, Box 3V224. Richards at the Black Leadership Summit with, (left to right), Texas State Rep. Jerald Larry (D-Dallas), Congresswoman Eddie Bernice Johnson (D-Dallas), and Texas State Sen. Rodney Ellis (D-Houston), Austin, Texas, August 18, 1990.

Page 100 Bob Daemmrich. Richards reflects on her

victory in the runoff election against Attorney General Jim Mattox, Hyatt Regency, Austin, Texas, April 10, 1990.

Pages 102–103 Ave Bonar. The Dolph Briscoe Center for American History, The University of Texas at Austin, Box 3V224. Richards meets Virgie (left) and her mother, Magnolia, fishing in a tributary of the Red River after attending a private fundraising luncheon outside Texarkana, Texas, March 12, 1990.

Pages 104–105 Ave Bonar. Photo 1991/185-63-22, Courtesy of Texas State Library and Archives Commission. At the inaugural ball held at Austin's Driskill Hotel, Richards and her escort, Edwin "Bud" Shrake, walk through the traditional arch of sabers held by members of the Ross Volunteers of Texas A&M University, January 15, 1991.

Pages 106–107 Lisa Davis. AR-2010-022-05-07-012, Austin History Center, Austin Public Library. Governor Ann Richards, with Queen Elizabeth II and Prince Philip, greeting spectators in front of the Texas Capitol during a historic royal visit to Texas, May 20, 1991. Austin Mayor Lee Cooke is on the right behind Richards.

Pages 108–109 Ave Bonar. The Dolph Briscoe Center for American History, The

University of Texas at Austin, Box 3V224. After a campaign rally at Trejo Hall in El Paso, Richards and her son Dan fly home to Austin, April 8, 1990.

Pages 110–111 Ave Bonar. Richards speaks at the National Women's Conference in Houston, Texas, November 19, 1977.

Pages 112–113 Photographer unknown. Richards (third from left) with fellow Girls Nation participants in front of the U.S. Supreme Court Building, Washington, D.C., ca. 1949.

Page 115 Bob Daemmrich. Richards reflects during a daylong campaign swing around the state, 1990.

Pages 116–117 Photographer unknown. Ann Richards Papers, di_07751, The Dolph Briscoe Center for American History, The University of Texas at Austin. Richards stands before the Austin skyline during her race for Travis County commissioner, 1976.

Pages 118–119 Ave Bonar. The Dolph Briscoe Center for American History, The University of Texas at Austin, Box 3V225. Richards reacts to an announcement made by Barbara Jordan, who had just told the crowd of supporters and the media that Richards's opponent, millionaire rancher and oilman Clayton Williams, had

140

admitted to reporters on a whistle-stop that day that he hadn't paid income tax in 1986. Richards, who released her tax returns, had repeatedly called for Williams to release his, and Williams refused. In the four remaining days of the race, the media focused on Williams's admission, which became the last major issue in the race, IBEW Hall, Houston, Texas, November 2, 1990.

Page 121 David J. Phillip. AP Photo. Texas Governor Ann Richards releases a raptor along the Rio Grande near Lajitas, Texas, 1993.

Pages 122–123 Ave Bonar. The Dolph Briscoe Center for American History, The University of Texas at Austin, Box 3V224. Former San Antonio Mayor Henry Cisneros and Texas State Rep. Wilhelmina Delco (far right) endorse Richards in the Democratic gubernatorial primary, Austin, Texas, February 24,1990.

Pages 124–125 Bob Thomas. UPI Photo. PICB-19739, Austin History Center, Austin Public Library. Richards casts her ballot on Election Day, November 2, 1982.

Page 127 Ave Bonar. The Dolph Briscoe Center for American History, The University of Texas at Austin, Box 3V224. Richards kicks off her campaign for governor with an environmental

awareness boat trip through the Gulf Intracoastal Waterway, August 30, 1989.

Pages 128–129 Ralph Barrera. AP Photo. Richards's eldest granddaughter, Lily Adams, delivers the eulogy at Richards's memorial service at the Frank Irwin Center in Austin, Texas, September 18, 2006.

Pages 130–131 Bob Daemmrich. Richards poses with the Texas state flag at one of the stops on a daylong campaign trip, 1990.

Page 133 Will van Overbeek for *Texas Monthly* magazine. Richards's chief speechwriter, Suzanne Coleman, at the Texas State Capitol, Austin, Texas, 1992.

Page 133 Ave Bonar. Holland Taylor performs at the Lincoln Center in her one-woman stage production, Ann, New York City, February 16, 2013. Taylor immersed herself in the starring role of her Tony-nominated play, which premiered in Galveston in 2010 and sold out in theaters across the country, including on Broadway and at the Kennedy Center in Washington, D.C. The play can be seen on the PBS Great Performances online platform.

Page 134 *Clockwise from top left:* **Casey Chapman Ross,** Austin; **Billy Calzada,** San Antonio; **Casey Chapman**

Ross, Austin; **Margaret Justus,** El Paso. Ann banners were displayed in various Texas cities throughout 2021.

Page 135 *Top:* **Ben Torres.** Dallas; *Bottom:* **John Burnett.** Houston, where Margaret Justus, founder of the Ann Richards Legacy Project, stands under an Ann banner.

Pages 136–137 Lisa Davis. AR-2010-022-05-07-012, Austin History Center, Austin Public Library. Richards with Willie Nelson at a campaign fundraiser, Austin Opera House, Austin, Texas, 1990.

Page 141 Bob Daemmrich. Newly sworn in Governor Richards gestures toward the crowd after giving her inaugural speech, Austin, Texas, January 15, 1991

Pages 142–143 Erich Schlegel. Richards shops for shoes in New York City while chair of the 1992 Democratic National Convention. Richards's press secretary, Margaret Justus (left), schedules multiple media appearances that week, New York City, July 1992.

Page 144 Paul Moseley. Courtesy of *Fort Worth Star-Telegram* Collection, Special Collections, The University of Texas at Arlington Libraries. Richards signs "Hook 'em" to celebrants on her inaugural parade horse-drawn-carriage ride along Congress Avenue, with son Dan and daughter Ellen, Austin, Texas, January 15, 1991.

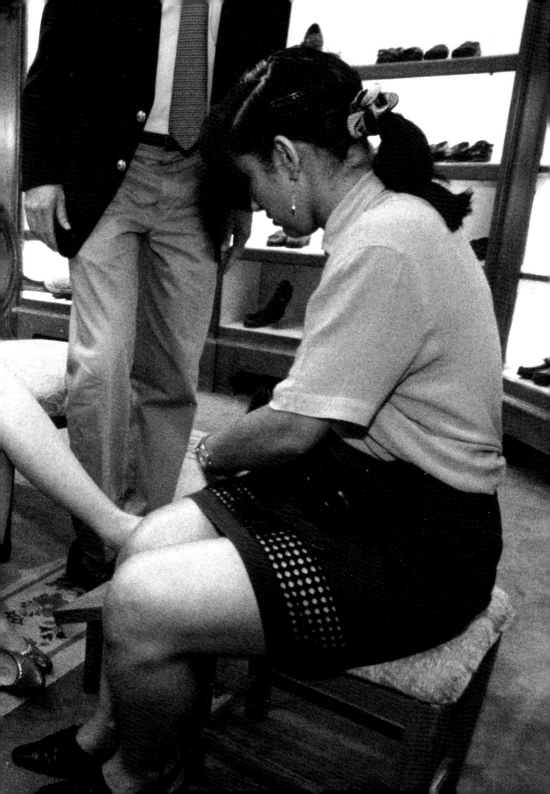